I0801015

CYCLES IN NATURE

WATER CYCLE

BY ANGELA LIM

Kids Core
An Imprint of Abdo Publishing
abdobooks.com

abdobooks.com

Published by Abdo Publishing, a division of ABDO, PO Box 398166, Minneapolis, Minnesota 55439.

Printed in the United States of America, North Mankato, Minnesota.
102025
012026

THIS BOOK CONTAINS RECYCLED MATERIALS

Cover Photo: Dmitry Pichugin/Shutterstock Images
Interior Photos: Shutterstock Images, 4–5, 9, 10, 12–13, 20–21, 26, 28–29; Josef Gabrhel/Shutterstock Images, 7; Ann Gaysorn/Shutterstock Images, 15; Serhii Sirochuk/Shutterstock Images, 17; Rudi Everaert/500px/Getty Images, 18; Gritsalak Karalak/Shutterstock Images, 22; J. J. Gouin/Shutterstock Images, 25

Editors: Rebecca Higgins and Trudy Becker
Series Designer: Katharine Hale

Library of Congress Control Number: 2025939181

Publisher's Cataloging-in-Publication Data

Names: Lim, Angela, author.
Title: Water cycle / by Angela Lim
Description: Minneapolis, Minnesota: Abdo Publishing, 2026 | Series: Cycles in nature | Includes online resources and index.
Identifiers: ISBN 9781098298678 (lib. bdg.) | ISBN 9798384932475 (ebook)
Subjects: LCSH: Water--Juvenile literature. | Water cycle--Juvenile literature. | Hydrologic cycle--Juvenile literature. | Natural cycle--Juvenile literature. | Ecological processes--Juvenile literature.
Classification: DDC 551.48--dc23

CONTENTS

Rain is part of the water cycle.

CHAPTER 1

IT'S POURING!

Beth and her family were going to spend the weekend at her grandparents' house. She was excited. But the car ride was long! And Beth was getting bored. She breathed on the glass, causing it to fog up. Then she drew a smiley face and watched it disappear.

"It looks like a storm is coming," Beth's dad said from the passenger seat. He pointed toward the windshield. Beth looked forward. Dark clouds were beginning to gather. It had been a warm summer day, but now it was getting cooler and gloomier. Tree branches shook as the wind picked up. Lightning flashed in the distance. Thunder rumbled.

Soon, large raindrops splattered on the windshield. Beth's mom flicked on the windshield wipers. A stream of water droplets raced across the windows. As the car crossed over a tall bridge, Beth noticed the rushing water far below.

The lightning and thunder stopped. But rain was still falling when Beth and her

Lightning is a spark of electricity. It can appear in the sky or between clouds and the ground. Thunder is the noise made by lightning.

parents arrived. Water rushed into the gutter at the end of her grandparents' street. Beth and her parents hurried indoors.

The next day was bright and sunny. As Beth walked around the neighborhood with her grandma, the sidewalks were dry. Only a few puddles remained.

The Water Cycle

Thunderstorms are possible because of the water cycle. The water cycle is the movement of

Water's Role

Water plays a huge role in daily life. People do not just drink water. It is also used for cooking and bathing. Plants, crops, and animals all need water to survive. Some cities even get their energy from water! Rivers rush through dams that create energy.

Puddles form when rain falls too quickly for it to soak into the ground.

water from Earth's surface to the **atmosphere** and back again. There are four main parts of the water cycle. They are evaporation, condensation, precipitation, and collection.

Hail is ice that falls from the sky.

About 71 percent of Earth's surface is covered in water. The oceans contain nearly 97 percent of Earth's water. The ice at the North and South Poles makes up about 2 percent of the water on Earth. Lakes, rivers, and streams are also sources of water. Some water is underground. All these sources of water go through the water cycle.

The water cycle is a constant and continuous process. Water changes form during this cycle. For example, water from the ocean changes from liquid to gas when it evaporates into the atmosphere. In the atmosphere, water forms droplets. The droplets form clouds. Water eventually falls back to Earth in liquid or solid form. It might return as rain, snow, or hail. The water cycle is important for life on Earth.

Explore Online

Visit the website below. Does it give any new information about the water cycle that was not in Chapter One?

What Is the Water Cycle?

abdocorelibrary.com/water-cycle

When water is heated in a pot to a temperature of 212 degrees Fahrenheit (100°C), it comes to a boil. Some of the boiling water changes from liquid to gas in the form of steam.

CHAPTER 2

IN THE ATMOSPHERE

One part of the water cycle is evaporation. This is the process of water changing from a liquid into a gas. Evaporation is similar to what happens when water boils. However, boiling is a rapid process. Evaporation in nature is a much slower process.

Water evaporates from oceans, lakes, rivers, and other bodies of water. The gas produced by evaporation is called water vapor. Unlike steam, water vapor is invisible to the human eye. Evaporation in nature can happen at any temperature. However, warmer temperatures can cause water to evaporate more quickly. Wind makes a difference too. Stronger wind speeds up evaporation.

Making Salt

Evaporation is one way to get table salt. When salt water evaporates, only the water becomes gas. The salt becomes **crystals**. Then people can gather the salt crystals and use them.

During hot summer months, gardeners might have to water their plants more often.

Humidity affects how quickly water evaporates too. When there is a lot of moisture in the air, evaporation occurs more slowly. Evaporation also affects humidity.

As water evaporates, it adds moisture to the air. About 90 percent of the moisture in the atmosphere comes from evaporation.

Transpiration is another way moisture enters the atmosphere. It occurs as plants lose water vapor through their leaves. Plant roots **absorb** water from the soil. Water moves through the plant. It is released as water vapor through small holes in the leaves called stomata.

Condensation

Condensation is the next stage in the water cycle. It is the process of gas transforming into a liquid. People can see condensation when water droplets collect on a cool glass of water. The droplets form as water vapor cools.

Dew is condensation. It makes grass wet when it has not rained.

Fog is a form of condensation.

In nature, condensation forms clouds. Water vapor rises. The upper parts of the atmosphere can be very cold. As the water vapor cools, it becomes liquid again.

A solid surface is needed for condensation to happen. The water droplets that make up clouds condense around tiny particles. These particles may be specks of dust, salt, or ash.

Condensation can also happen close to Earth's surface. It forms fog. Fog is like a cloud close to the ground. Humidity is necessary for fog to form. When cold air and warm air mix together at high humidity, the water vapor in warm air cools. The vapor becomes liquid, creating fog.

Further Evidence

Look at the website below. Does it give any new evidence to support Chapter Two?

The Water Cycle!

abdocorelibrary.com/water-cycle

The temperature must be 32 degrees Fahrenheit (0°C) or colder for snow to form.

CHAPTER 3

FALLING BACK TO EARTH

An important stage in the water cycle is precipitation. This is when water in the atmosphere returns to Earth's surface. Precipitation occurs in several forms. Snow, rain, and hail are examples of precipitation.

Winter Precipitation

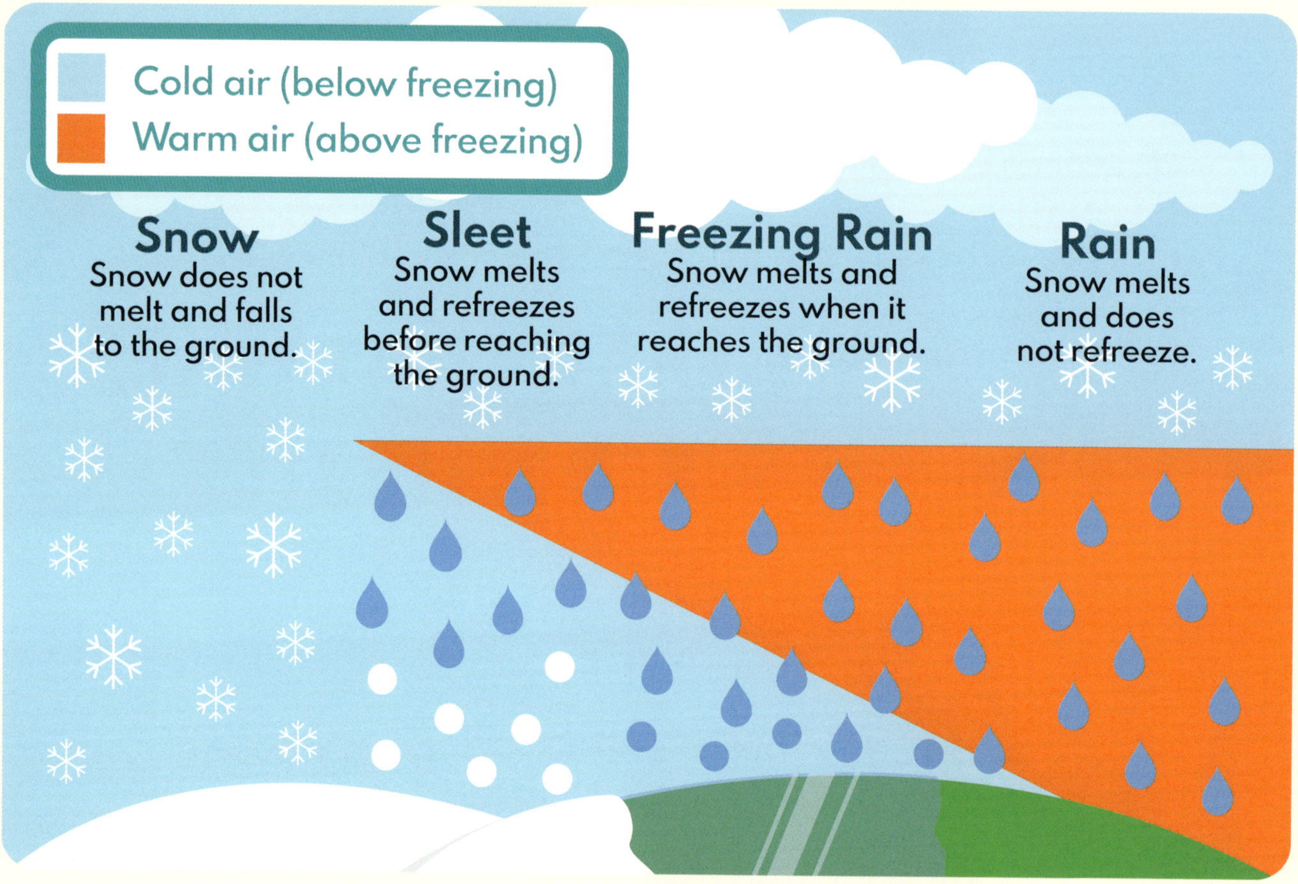

Different types of precipitation can occur during winter. The type of precipitation depends on the air temperature as water droplets fall from clouds.

Precipitation begins in clouds. As clouds form, water droplets run into each other. This causes the droplets to grow in size and weight.

Water droplets in clouds are tiny. It takes millions of cloud droplets to form a single raindrop. Finally, when droplets become too heavy, they fall from the cloud.

In extreme cold, precipitation may happen even before clouds form. In this case, water vapor cools quickly and crystallizes. Gas changes directly into a solid. The ice crystals become snowflakes.

Collection and Runoff

The water cycle continues after precipitation returns water to Earth's surface. Some of that water is collected in bodies of water. It joins rivers, lakes, oceans, and more. Other water is absorbed into the ground.

Water droplets fill the space between soil particles. This water is called groundwater. Still other water flows over the land. That is called runoff. Eventually, runoff gathers in lakes, rivers, and other bodies of water.

Some runoff flows downhill and picks up dirt and other **sediment**. Runoff shapes the landscape. It causes **erosion** as it carries soil from one place to another.

Rainfall around the World

The Atacama Desert is in northern Chile. It is the driest place on Earth. Parts of the desert get less than 0.03 inches (1 mm) of rainfall each year. Mawsynram is in northeastern India. The town is one of Earth's wettest places. It gets almost 470 inches (1,934 cm) of rain each year!

As runoff flows, it can pick up things that make water dirty. People can use fewer chemicals in their yards and gardens to help keep bodies of water clean.

Different parts of the water cycle affect each other. For example, heavy rain creates more runoff. This is because the rain falls too quickly for the soil to absorb it.

Water easily erodes soft rock. It takes longer to erode harder rock.

Soil type affects erosion. Soil that doesn't absorb much water is easily washed away. Plant life is another factor that affects erosion. Thick plants slow erosion.

Plants and people depend on the water cycle. Everyone can help the water cycle by saving water. People can try to use less water. Gardeners can collect rainwater for their plants. Saving water in these ways helps it stay in the water cycle.

PRIMARY SOURCE

Environmental scientist Debbie Archer wrote about the water cycle. She said:

> By being responsible with the water we do have, we can make sure it's there when we need it. Additionally, if we **pollute** the water we have, we are making it unusable for a very long time. Clean, fresh water is important for all living things.

Source: Debbie Archer. "The Water Cycle Revisited!" *Audubon Vermont*, 9 June 2020, vt.audubon.org. Accessed 9 Apr. 2025.

Comparing Texts

Think about the quote. Does it give the same perspective as the chapter or a different one? Explain how in a few sentences.

CYCLE SUMMARY

Precipitation is how water in the atmosphere returns to Earth's surface.

Collection is when water is stored in its liquid form.

Condensation is when gas becomes liquid.
Evaporation is the transformation of water from liquid into gas.

Glossary

absorb
to take in

atmosphere
the layer of gas surrounding Earth

crystals
solid objects whose structures have a repeating pattern

erosion
the process of land being moved or broken down by water, wind, and ice

humidity
the amount of water in the air

pollute
to make impure, usually with chemicals or waste

sediment
particles moved by water, wind, or ice

Online Resources

To learn more about the water cycle, visit our free resource websites below.

Core Library CONNECTION
FREE! COMMON CORE MULTIMEDIA RESOURCES

Visit **abdocorelibrary.com** or scan this QR code for free Common Core resources for teachers and students, including vetted activities, multimedia, and booklinks, for deeper subject comprehension.

Booklinks NONFICTION NETWORK
FREE! ONLINE NONFICTION RESOURCES

Visit **abdobooklinks.com** or scan this QR code for free additional online weblinks for further learning. These links are routinely monitored and updated to provide the most current information available.

Learn More

Buckey, A. W. *Weather.* Abdo, 2025.

Hayes, Madeline J. *How Does Water Move Around?* Flowerpot, 2023.

Water Cycles. DK, 2021.

Index

About the Author

Angela Lim is an MFA student in poetry at Indiana University.